ROLLER SKATING
by Joseph F. Shevelson

HARVEY HOUSE, PUBLISHERS • NEW YORK, NEW YORK

This book is dedicated to America's most wholesome family sport.

This book could not have been written without the work and intelligence of George Werner, Irwin N. Rosee and the dedicated staff of the Roller Skating Foundation of America, Fred Down, Budd Van Roekel and George Pickard, the officers of the RSROA, the staff of the RSROA, Harry Harris (chief sports photographer of the Associated Press), Gordon Ware and Robert Ware Jr., and the staff of the Chicago Roller Skate Company — and above all, James Leonard Plimpton who invented the modern roller skate.

The author wishes to acknowledge the Nassau County Department of Recreation and Parks, Mineola, L.I., America on Wheels, Marvin Facher, and Marvin Kanengiser for their assistance.

Copyright © 1978 by Harvey House, Publishers

All rights reserved, including the right
to reproduce this book or portions thereof in any form.

Library of Congress Catalog Card Number 78-56557
Manufactured in the United States of America
ISBN 0-8178-5944-6

Published in Canada by Fitzhenry & Whiteside, Ltd., Toronto

Harvey House, Publishers
20 Waterside Plaza, New York, New York 10010

CONTENTS

CHAPTER ONE • HISTORY

Roller skating today is a recognized sport and popular recreation. Millions of youngsters skate just for the pure fun of it. There are over 5,000 commercial roller rinks throughout the United States and Canada, and thousands more throughout the world. Many clubs, schools, churches and municipal recreation centers have roller skating programs. There are colleges which give physical education credits for roller skating. Many levels of competition exist for interested skaters. This is an established sport with a new popularity.

The history of roller skating extends over a period of more than two hundred years.

Roller skates, which sometimes have been called 'Wheel Skates' and at one time were called 'Parlor Skates,' originated during the early 1700s in the Netherlands where everyone was ice-skating minded, even in the summertime. The first roller skates were made by attaching wooden spools to strips of wood nailed to a pair of wooden shoes. This enabled the Dutch to skate even in the summertime when the canals were not frozen.

An etching from 1877 depicting young girls performing "The Chase of the Butterfly" at the Brooklyn, New York Skating Rink.

Probably the most important event in roller skating history occurred in 1863 when J. L. Plimpton of New York introduced the parent of all present-day roller skates. His improved skate had two pairs of boxwood wheels geared so that the skates would turn when the foot plate was tilted to either side. The skate worked on spring-like rubber pads.

In 1864, Everett H. Barney of Springfield, Massachusetts, began to market roller skates and his was the first roller skate sold to the American public. In 1866 Plimpton opened the first roller skating rink in the United States at Newport, Rhode Island while continuing work on his skate,

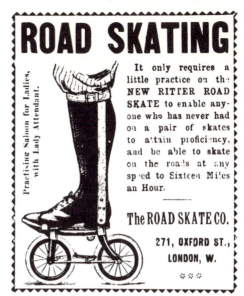

(Right) An advertisement from 1897 for an English Road Skate. (Below left) J. L. Plimpton, father of the modern roller skate. (Below right) A drawing from Plimpton's 1863 patent of his "Parlor Skate."

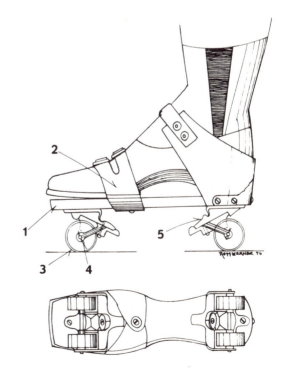

making many improvements and taking out new patents until, in 1874, he introduced a skate that is very similar to the ones in use today.

Late in the same year that Plimpton first devised his mechanical principle, A. F. Smith of Chicago introduced another revolutionary idea, the pin bearing. This improvement allowed the wheels to turn more easily than had been possible before. Smith became quite an expert on his skates and after a few years, in 1882, he gave a demonstration at the Casino Rink in Chicago, before an audience of more than 3,000 people. His exhibition contained more than two hundred fancy figures and gave a good indication of the possibilities of the sport.

In the same year, the Polo League, made up of teams from seven midwestern cities, was formed. They played games such as pushball, basketball and polo on roller skates and had sprint races and high jumping contests. Roller skating even went so far as to have marathons. There is a record of a typical six-day roller race at New York City's Madison Square Garden in 1884 which was won by a man named Donovan. He skated 1,091 miles to victory!

Today there are associations for the amateur skater and there are nearly twenty million skaters who skate under supervised programs in indoor rinks. There are millions more who skate in school yards, streets, sidewalks and gymnasiums without programs.

There are dozens of types of roller skates to serve this great mass of skaters. Today there are roller skates available for street and rink skaters from a basic skate costing five dollars a pair to sophisticated types which sell for over one hundred dollars a pair. Even with its great popularity there is every indication that roller skating will grow as a sport and recreation.

J. L. Plimpton could never have imagined what he was starting when he perfected his first modern skate.

CHAPTER TWO • SKATES AND SAFETY

It's a far cry from the first skate patented by James Plimpton in 1863 to the present-day roller skate, a thing of beauty and a triumph of engineering achievement.

Plimpton made dance and figure skating possible on roller skates by mounting two parallel sets of boxwood wheels against rubber pads so that skaters could turn with ease simply by shifting weight.

But like the difference between the 'tin lizzie' and the modern, stream-lined automobile, there has been vast progress in roller skate manufacturing from Plimpton's era to the present.

Now roller skates roll off the assembly line by the millions. But, thanks to modern techniques and precision engineering, each pair is a world away from the make-shift affairs that Plimpton fashioned by hand from improvised materials and with inadequate tools.

Today, there's a skate for every skater, depending upon his or her ability, budget and special needs or preferences.

In the selection of roller skates for any purpose, the following is a list of considerations in order of their importance:

1. **ACTION:** How the skate responds to the skater shifting his or her

weight and leaning. This is the key to performance and maneuverability. The skate action can be **single rubber** for more stability as needed in racing or hockey skates, or **double rubber** for quicker or more responsive action as needed in figure and free style skates. Also, skate action can be 45 degrees for a lower, more stable skate (racing) or 10 degrees for a more responsive skate (figure).

2. **COMFORT:** How the skate and/or shoe-skate fit and feel in use.

3. **DURABILITY:** How long the skate should last without major replacement or repairs.

4. **APPEARANCE:** How attractive is the skate and/or shoe-skate? How much work is needed to maintain them?

5. **COST:** The real value of a pair of skates depends to a large degree upon the amount of use and the degree of maintenance.

The major features of the modern roller skate are shown below.

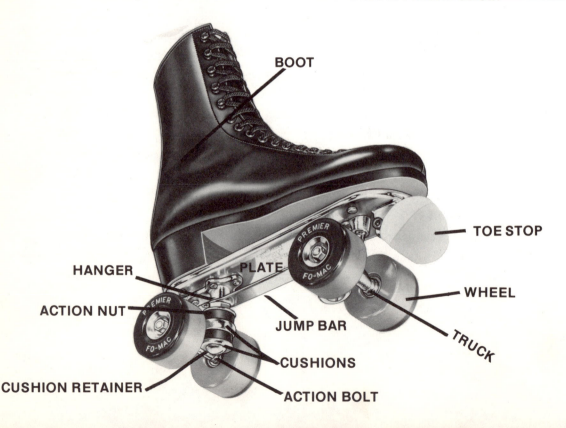

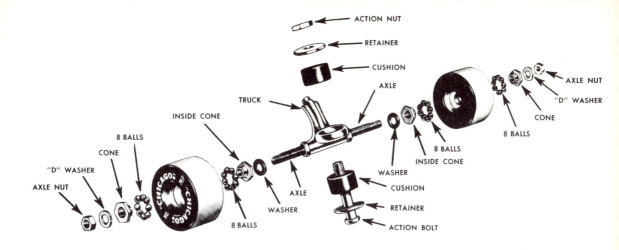

ACTION NUT

RETAINER

CUSHION

AXLE

TRUCK

INSIDE CONE

8 BALLS

CONE

"D" WASHER

AXLE NUT

AXLE

WASHER

8 BALLS

WASHER

CUSHION

RETAINER

ACTION BOLT

INSIDE CONE

8 BALLS

AXLE NUT

"D" WASHER

CONE

8 BALLS

The components of the wheel and truck assembly are shown above.

There are many features of roller skates that vary in regard to their use and price level. Here is a brief summary of skate components and how they vary:

1. **PLATES:** This is the foot plate that attaches to the shoe and holds the action assembly which in turn holds the wheel. It can be steel, cast-aluminum, drop-forged aluminum or fiberglass.

2. **TRUCKS:** This is the part that attaches to the plate and holds the axle and wheels. Trucks are either malleable iron, cast aluminum or fiberglass. They turn in response to weight that compresses an action rubber cushion (or two cushions in the case of double rubber action skates). This is the action of a skate and the very heart of its performance and durability.

3. **TOE STOPS:** This is the rubber bumper that fits on the toe of the skate for the dual purpose of protecting the shoe and serving as a brake and a platform for jumps and spins in figure skating. Most skates today have toe stops built-in as an integral part of the plate.

4. **WHEELS:** This is obviously an important part of a skate and its action. Most wheels have been made of a compression-molded combination of rubber and plastic. Recently, wheels made of polyurethane have become popular. Urethane wheels have the advantage of excellent traction, tremendous wear and good appearance. However, they have the disadvantage of being hard to push. There is constant experimentation with other materials in search of the perfect roller skate wheels.

There are three basic categories of wheel construction. (1) **Precision** refers to any wheel that contains precision-ground ball bearings. These wheels are used for better skates since they provide a smooth, almost frictionless roll. (2) **Semi-precision** wheels are found on medium priced skates. They have a retained ring of balls with a standard bushing. ("Bushing" is a metallic lining designed to prevent rubbing between the bearings.) Thus, any standard wheel can be made semi-precision by adding bearings in a retainer ring and a special semi-precision cone. (3) **Loose-ball** refers to any wheel (usually found on road and racing skates) containing standard bushing and cones and a complement of steel ball bearings (16 per wheel) without a retainer. The bearings roll freely between the wheel bushing and cone.

Below, the major parts of the wheel and truck assembly.

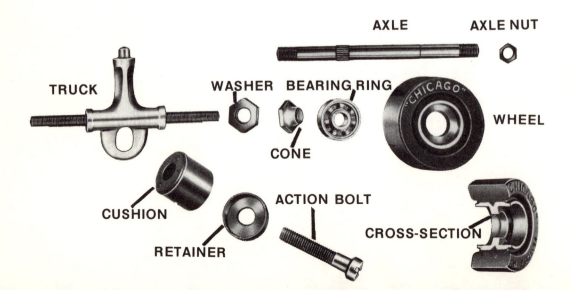

AXLE AXLE NUT

TRUCK WASHER BEARING RING "CHICAGO" WHEEL

CONE

CUSHION ACTION BOLT

RETAINER CROSS-SECTION

Since there are several categories in the sport of roller skating (Dance, Figure, Free Style, Speed, Hockey) there are several types of skates. Certain features (action, wheel, shoe) are preferred for each kind of skate.

Figure or Free Style Skates are built for smooth roll and quick response. They have 10 degree double rubber action with larger wheels that roll smoothly and quietly on precision ground bearings. Figure and free style skates always have adjustable toe stops.

Racing Skates are built low and lightweight for stability and speed. They usually have 45 degree action with wheels that are smaller and designed to combine traction with easy roll. In America, racing skates have adjustable, wide toe stops to provide a platform when racers start a race. In Australia and many other parts of the world, toe stops are not allowed on racing skates.

Dance Skates are the same as figure or free style skates, but the wheels are slightly smaller and toe stops are not used.

Hockey Skates are usually the same as racing skates, but the wheels are designed more for traction and less for easy roll. The main difference is in the shoe. Hockey shoes are similar to ice hockey shoes and are therefore more durable and offer more protection than the lightweight racing shoe.

Road Skates are newly developed skates for use on sidewalk, bike paths and paved roads. They are being used wherever there are joggers or cyclists. The main difference from other skates is in the wheel which is larger, softer and of special high rebound urethane with precision bearings. These wheels cushion the roll over cracks, pebbles and uneven pavement.

In summary, the quality features of any roller skate depend on how you use them and how much you care to spend. There is always available a good-better-best skate for each use. A qualified dealer would know best what skate is right for your needs and budget.

MAINTENANCE

The care of a skate's wheels involves adjustment and lubrication.

There should be a slight amount of shake or play in wheel adjustment. The inner cone should be drawn hard and fast against a lock washer at the end of the truck. It should remain in this position for the life of the skate or until the cone needs replacing. The outside cone is adjustable. For proper adjustment, turn the outer cone down until it sets on the ball bearing. Then back it off one-third of a turn. This will leave a slight play between bearings, cones and bushings. This spacing allows for heat expansion in use.

16

Ball bearing wheels should be oiled at least once a month with one drop of oil on each side of the wheel. Precision bearing wheels can be oiled monthly, or the bearings should be packed with a good grade of channeling grease. If the grease hardens, bearings should be cleaned in a cleaning solvent and repacked.

There are a few simple rules for the care of skates.

1. Store skates in a dry place.

2. Check adjustments and secureness of wheels-action assembly and toe stops on a regular basis.

3. Clean and lubricate skates regularly.

4. Rotate, grind and change wheels whenever necessary.

5. Replace parts as soon as they show signs of wear.

6. Be alert for loose nuts, missing balls, wheels with flat spots and worn or loose toe stops.

Roller skating is a safe and enjoyable sport as long as simple guidelines are followed.

Outdoor Guidelines

1. Demonstrate courtesy when skating on sidewalk.

2. Give pedestrians the right of way.

3. Observe local laws pertaining to roller skating on sidewalks.

4. Do not race out of blind driveways or alleys.

5. Avoid skating on chipped, broken and rough areas. Watch out for natural hazards such as rocks, branches or trees.

6. Come to a complete stop and look in all directions before crossing street intersections. If there is heavy traffic, remove your skates and walk to a safe place.

7. Avoid uncontrolled coasting and skating down steep inclines.

8. Never hitch onto bicycles, mopeds, autos or trucks.

9. Never skate faster than you know you can control.

Indoor Guidelines

1. When entering the skating floor the right of way is always given to skaters already on the floor.

2. When leaving the skating floor, move slowly to your right, well ahead of your exit so that you will not be cutting across the path of other skaters.

3. Skate only in the direction of the general skating traffic.

4. Do not skate fast, push or play tag.

5. If you fall, get up as quickly as possible, preferably facing oncoming traffic.

6. Be alert to those around you. Tripping over someone who has fallen could bring serious injury to yourself and others.

CHAPTER THREE • THE RINK

There are over 5,000 commercial indoor roller rinks in the United States and Canada which offer ideal conditions for the enjoyment of roller skating.

These include a large skating surface which is kept in excellent shape, music and lighting systems which provide a variety of moods, shoe-skates which can be rented for a small fee and game and party rooms for groups. Almost all such rinks have concession stands similar to those found in motion picture theatres or sports arenas.

Although independently owned, the rinks are bound together by a network of organizations which urges the owners to empahsize "good wholesome fun for the family" in their own best financial interests. These organizations include the Chicago Roller Skate Company, which sells about 90% of the shoe-skates sold in America, and the Roller Skating Rink Operators Association, with main headquarters in Lincoln, Nebraska, which offers guidelines to its members for successful management and promotion.

19

As the disc jockey looks on, a line of skaters try out the 'disco bump.'

The main difference between 'street' and 'rink' skating is the skating surface itself. Skating surfaces in indoor rinks range upward in size from a 'small' area of about 150 by 75 feet. This free skating area provides the skater with the opportunity to concentrate on skills which would be impossible to develop in the streets of a city.

The music and lighting provide different moods which are varied for public skating sessions and/or party groups at the discretion of the skaters and managers. The shoe-skates available for rental are of good quality and are maintained by an expert. The concession stand gives you the opportunity of having a snack or just taking a rest from all the exhilaration and excitement.

20

Naturally, when 200 to 400 persons are skating in a relatively confined area, it is necessary to establish rules. All commercial rinks, therefore, have floor guards who direct and control the flow of the skating and a set of rules which are strictly enforced to ensure the safety of all skaters.

The commonly-accepted dress of the community is permitted at almost all rinks.

Commercial rinks offer a wide variety of programs designed for children as young as six and senior citizens past retirement age. Most rinks have established tie-ins with such organizations as the Girl and Boy Scouts, 4-H Clubs, Campfire Girls as well as school and church groups which skate in private sessions. The rinks also offer skating programs for housewives (so-called 'Slim Chick Clubs') and the entire family at special rates.

A certain percentage of 'occasional skaters' become hooked on roller skating and want to go beyond the basic skills of moving forward and backward, turning and staying off the floor. For these, rinks provide the opportunity to improve on one's ability for sheer enjoyment or, for a dedicated few, to go on to regional, national and even international competition.

No one could possibly learn such skills, whether in artistic, speed or hockey, without instruction. Rinks, therefore, have teaching professionals available for those skaters who wish to climb the performance ladder. At what point the skater stops climbing the ladder — the club or the regional, national or international competitive level — is up to the individual.

Skating surfaces in indoor rinks are maple hardwood, particle board, asphalt, concrete and terrazo (flooring made of small pieces of stone set in concrete). By far the most popular surface, however, is the maple hardwood surface. It provides the best possible surface and is tremendously durable when properly maintained. There is a rink in Pennsylvania, for example, which has a maple hardwood surface in excellent condition although it is over 50 years old.

Roller rinks in the 1950s and 1960s were traditional in music and decor — with an organ providing the music and simple lighting. By the mid-1960s, most rinks had music amplified over powerful speakers. Promotion-conscious managers of these commercial rinks have responded to the changing attitudes of our society by substituting sophisticated stereo systems for the organ, and the disco beat for the sounds of the 1950s and early 1960s.

And now — **Disco Skate**, utilizing flashing colored lights and highly professional sound equipment, has brought teenagers and those in their early twenties back to the rink. People are even learning how to do 'The Hustle,' 'Disco Tango,' and other dancesteps on skates. 'Going to the local rink' has taken on a whole new meaning with a new generation of skaters brought up on Rock-and-Roll and **Saturday Night Fever.**

Left, a skater, at rest, looks over the rink. Right, can you 'hustle' on skates? These two disco skaters, in motion, prove you can.

CHAPTER FOUR • A SPORT OF MANY SKILLS

One reason roller skating is enjoyable is that you can continually learn new maneuvers, regardless how often you put on the skates. Let's talk about some of these maneuvers and how to perform them.

When first you put on a pair of skates, you will notice that to go forward is quite different from walking. In walking, you progress by placing one foot in front of the other and transferring your weight by stepping down on one foot while lifting the other foot.

In skating, you move forward by placing one foot on the floor alongside the other and then by pushing sideways and backwards with the foot that had already been on the floor. This sideways pushing is always used in skating no matter how advanced you become.

After you have pushed with one foot, take it off the floor so you are balancing on one foot. Stand up as straight as you can to keep your balance over the skate on the floor. If you bend your knees just a little, you will find it is easier to keep your balance.

Now try to move forward on the other foot. Just as before, place the foot that is off the floor alongside the one that is on the floor and use the one that was on the floor to push sideways and backward. There you have the method used to skate forward. As long as you roller skate, you will use the same method.

Having started to skate forward, we need next to learn how to stop. You have probably noticed already that whether you have two feet on the floor or one, all four wheels of your skate roll at the same time in the same direction. In order to stop, we make the wheels go sideways. Since they cannot roll sideways, they stop us. So, if we want to stop, we stand on one foot and turn the other foot sideways while it is in the air; then lower it to the floor right at the heel of the foot already on the floor.

Follow the sequence of photographs from the top of this page to the bottom to see stopping in action. Your two feet, at the moment you stop, should form a **T** with the back foot sliding on the floor sideways. As you practice this, you will find you can stop with more efficiency.

After you can comfortably place your foot down and stop, it is time to consider how to start with nothing to assist you. If you leave your feet in the position for stopping — that is, one foot facing the direction you want to go and the other sideways to it — you need only push the sideways foot backward and the other foot will move you forward. Ths is the way we can get started in a hurry without grabbing on to anything (or anybody).

An interesting thing about roller skates is that they are designed and built so that they can go forward or backward and curve at the same time. This skating of curves is called **skating edges.** The way you do this is lean your body in the direction you want to curve. The lean occurs from the foot, meaning you do not just lean the top of your body but rather all of it from the ankle up. When you lean to the left, regardless of which foot you are standing on, your skate will roll to the left. The same thing applies when you lean to the right except that the skate will glide toward the right. This maneuver, which we will call the **leaning turn,** is used to get around corners or to change the direction you are going.

There will be times when you will want to change direction fairly quickly and the leaning turn won't get you around as fast as you would like. There is a maneuver you can do called the **cutting the circle turn.** You begin just as though you were going to do the leaning turn by stepping on the left foot and leaning to the left — for a left turn, of course. Now, instead of then putting the right foot on the floor alongside the left, bring the right foot forward and cross it over in front of the left and then put it on the floor, continuing to lean to the left.

You are then ready to begin all over. Start again by placing the left foot forward on the floor while leaning. This turn will really get you around fast. In fact, it is basically what speed skaters do when they want to go around a turn at high speed.

Now that you can — hopefully — start, stop, skate forward and go around a turn, it is time to consider turning around and then skating backward. To turn around you use a turn called the **mohawk turn.** Follow the sequence of photos down this page and across the next to see how this turn works. The mohawk turn uses both feet, one at a time, to rotate your body.

Begin by skating forward on your right foot. Instead of bringing the left foot alongside the right and placing it on the floor going forward, turn the left foot around so that it is facing backward. This is the **spread eagle** position, so called because one foot faces forward while the other faces backward. As soon as the left foot is turned, place it on the floor and lift the right foot off the floor. You will notice that the left foot strikes the floor going backward.

28

The next part of the turn is made by bringing your right foot alongside the left and then placing it on the floor going backward. The left foot is then lifted off and turned in the air so that it is able to be put on the floor going forward again. You will see that it takes four steps to make this turn and you went from forward to backward and then forward again. The **mohawk turn**, with many variations, is the basic turn used in all phases of serious skating.

Since the **mohawk turn** gets you backward, you should know how to continue to **skate backward** instead of immediately turning to forward. Think back to how you made your skates move forward. You place one foot on the floor while pushing the other foot sideways and backward to propel yourself forward.

Now you are skating on one foot backward. Place the other foot on the floor alongside the first. The foot that is going to leave the floor is pushed sideways and in front which propels you backward on the other foot. Thus, if you make the **mohawk turn** and find yourself going backward on the right foot, you can continue going backward by placing the left foot alongside the right (still facing backward) then push the right foot sideways and forward. You can continue to go backward for as many steps as you desire. Whenever you want to again go forward, you need only turn the foot that is off the floor until it is facing forward and place it on the floor in that direction and finish another **mohawk turn.**

There is a game you can play which will also serve as an exercise to help you practice what we have just discussed. It is called the **Figure 8** and is designed to let you try many maneuvers in a small space. At the beginning you might want to draw two circles on the ground about 10 to 15 feet in diameter. These circles should join each other at some point. For a beginning game, start where the two circles join each other and skate into the right circle on the right foot, leaning to the right. See if you can make your skate follow the line around to where you begin. If the skate isn't turning enough, lean more — if it is turning too much, lean less.

When you get back to where you started, change feet and skate in the left circle with the left foot. By practicing this, you will quickly learn to control the lean of your body to make whatever leaning turn you wish. The next thing to try is to skate the right circle with the left foot, followed by the left circle with the right foot. Once again, you will find that you lean to the right to make your skate go right and lean to the left to make your skate go left.

The **cutting the circle turn** can now be tried in the **figure 8.** Begin skating in the left circle by stepping on the left foot while leaning to the left. Then cross the right foot over while still following the circle to the left. Repeat this as many times as is necessary to get back to where you started. Then skate into the right circle on the right foot. The left foot is now brought forward and crossed over the right. Again, repeat the steps following the circle until you get back to where the two circles join. You can make the circles as large or small as you desire. What you are learning is control — that means the ability to make your skates go where you want them to.

One great way to have fun is to try some **tricks.** You can do this after you learn how to start, stop, turn and have some control of your skates. The first one we'll consider is the **jump.** Jumping on roller skates is very similar to jumping without skates. When first attempting to jump, mark a line on the ground and plan to start your jump at that line. First, start a distance back from the line and build up speed, then put both feet on the ground and crouch by bending your knees, as shown to the right.

When you reach the line, push up with your legs, which will lift you into the air. Bend your legs while you are in the air and land on both legs at the same time. After finding you are able to jump close to the line each time, place a small cardboard box at the line and try to jump over it. As your skill improves, you can use even larger boxes, but always be sure they are made of material that won't hurt you if you miss. There are many variations on the jump, such as landing on one foot instead of two, holding your hands out during the jump, even eventually learning to turn your body in the air while jumping. By these complicated and possibly dangerous jumps should be left, for now, to experts like Peter McArthur, who is shown on this page in a flat-out jump during competition. For the daring, variations on the basic jump can come later — when you are comfortable and confident on your skates.

As you can see, there are many maneuvers in skating. Each time you learn how to do a maneuver, there is another one ready to be done using the skills you learned in the first maneuver. You'll find that roller skating will never get boring no matter how many times you put on skates.

Another fun trick is to **spin.** This means making your body act like a top and go round while you are in one place. Begin this trick almost the same way you began the mohawk turn; that is, step forward on your right foot, lift the left foot and turn it around in the air so it is pointed backward. At this point begin the spin by putting the left foot on the ground without taking up the right foot. Note here that the two legs tend to bring your two feet together, heel to heel, one skating forward, the other backward. As soon as you are in this position, draw your legs and arms in as much as you can and your spin circle will begin. The tighter you can draw in your arms, the faster the spin will go. By relaxing your legs and then pulling them together you can pump the spin to make it go faster.

As you learn to do the spin comfortably, you can alternate from two feet on the floor to lifting the right foot off for awhile. You will notice that as soon as you are standing on one foot, the spin will get faster. When practicing the spin, try to focus your eyes on an object some distance away. This will help to keep you from getting dizzy or falling. In advanced skating, the same spin is done but different leg and arm positions make it appear that the skaters are doing many different types of spin.

A skater 'in limbo.' The object of the game is to crouch low enough to pass under a bar without hitting it.

CHAPTER FIVE • FUN IN MANY FORMS

Skating is fun. One reason for this is that there are many kinds of games and activites that can be tried regardless where you do your skating. It is only necessary to know how to skate forward, move backward, and stop in order to take part in any game that your imagination can create.

Some activites come to mind immediately; **hockey** is one. This requires some extra equipment such as sticks and either a ball or a puck in order to get started.

Tag is a game that can be played with any number of friends. One version uses a hat as a target. A player is given the hat. The player who is 'it' chases the player with the hat, trying to tag him before he can pass the hat to another player. Any player tagged while holding the hat becomes 'it.' As you can see, you could use many different objects and still have fun.

Another way to have fun while skating is to have an **obstacle course race.** Simply decide on a course for the race such as a section of school yard or a large sidewalk area. Then place many different objects such as boxes, milk cartons, tin cans, or — as in the photograph — trash cans on the course in such a way that to get from one end to the other you have to skate in and out of the objects. The course can be laid out in chalk as well, if some is handy. Remember to pick up your obstacles when you are finished.

If you happen to be skating in a rink, many varieties of games can be attempted using the music system of the rink. For example, the rink can have four numbers hung from the ceiling. While the music plays, everyone skates around. When the music stops, everyone stops under one of the four numbers. Someone draws one of the four numbers out of a hat and everyone under that number leaves the floor. The game then continues with the music again. The form of musical chairs can end by having one winner or many, depending how long you wish to play.

By the use of your imagination, you can develop new games that could be played in limited space as well as in open area. **Follow the leader,** for example, can be adopted for skating with each person taking the leader's place for one round. When a person fails to **follow the leader** the leader gets a point. At the end of the game, the person who has earned the most points as a leader, is the winner.

One way to improve your skating ability and have fun at the same time is to make a game out of practicing how to start, skating forward in the direction you want, skating backward and stopping.

For instance, draw a line to be used as a 'starting line.' Then draw another line about ten feet (approximately four meters) away to be used as a finish line. Select one of your friends to act as referee. Everyone else stands on the line and when the referee says "Start" everyone gives one push toward the finish line. The object is to see who can skate on one foot from the start line to the finish line and stop closest to the line. The closest gets a point each time. The farthest from the stop line becomes the next referee.

So you can see that there are no limits to the fun you can have with games on skates. Almost any game that is played on your feet (football, baseball, basketball, frisbee, soccer, for example) can be adapted for skating. Therefore, all you need is a pair of skates — and your imagination.

Above, Merit Patches which can be earned by passing the skill tests administered by the A.A.U. and the U.S.A.C.

Right, a Boy Scout taking the obstacle course test.

CHAPTER SIX • TESTING SKATING SKILLS

We have discussed many different maneuvers that can be done on roller skates with just a small amount of practice. Naturally, the more you do these maneuvers, the better you will be able to do them and, as you get better, you will achieve a level of personal satisfaction from knowing how well you can perform each maneuver in comparison to how you previously could do it.

One other way that you can measure your progress in roller skating is to take a test that will determine your skill and accomplishments from the very basic maneuvers on up to very fancy and sophisticated skating.

Many organizations give tests and award certificates, ribbons, medals, badges and other forms of acknowledgement of your skill. For example, the Girl Scouts, the Boy Scouts, 4-H Clubs and Campfire Girls have tests for roller skating included in their badge programs. These tests consist primarily of seeing whether you can — unaided — start, stop, skate forward on one foot, skate backward and turn. Each test is slightly different, but all attempt to give you some indication as to how your skills are progressing. If you are now a member of these organizations or plan to become a member, you will have a chance to take their test as a part of their program.

Both the Amateur Athletic Union and USAC have developed a physical fitness test for roller skaters that requires the skater to do six maneuvers out of a possible twelve and for which they award a one-star patch (pictured on page 38). This test is usually given in a skating rink and is supervised by the test director or the professional skating teacher.

These tests are designed to test your ability to perform basic maneuvers in a different form. For instance, **skate the slalom** is a test to see if you can control your skates, making them go left or right so that you don't knock down (or run into) a series of pylons, flags or obstacles which are arranged to form a curved path. Ths is a test of the maneuver **leaning turn** which was described in Chapter Four.

The **shuttle skate** tests your ability to skate around a prescribed course while picking up a block (or another object), carrying it a certain distance, then placing it down in a designated area. All of this is done without stopping or dropping the block. You get the chance to test your ability to bend and straighten up while skating without losing your balance.

Remember the **figure 8** we described in Chapter Four? One of the AAU tests is the ability to perform the **figure 8** either following a line or making your own circles. For the adventurous, try doing it skating backward.

Earlier, we learned about a turn called the **mohawk turn.** To make this turn, you began on one foot skating forward, then turned the other foot in the air so it was placed on the floor rolling backward. In the AAU or USAC test, you have an opportunity to perform a variation on the turn called the **spread eagle** turn.

You begin on one foot skating forward, then turn the other foot in the air exactly the way you did for the mohawk turn. Then place the turned foot on the surface while the first foot stays on the ground. Thus, two feet will be on the floor — one facing in one direction and the other in the opposite direction. Since you will be rolling, one skate is rolling forward and the other is rolling backward. The AAU test is to see how far you can roll in this position.

The **spin** we described earlier is another of the AAU or USAC tests. The object of this test is to turn in the spin for a certain number of turns.

Shoot the Duck is a maneuver also used in the tests. This is a fun trick and tests your ability to maintain your balance on one foot while in a sitting position. You begin the exercise by sitting down on your skates while rolling forward. You then take one foot off the floor and hold it off so that it is out in front of you. After you have practiced this position a few times, you will find that you can start to master control of the skate on the ground so that you can follow a prescribed course which includes skating a zig-zag marked by flags or pylons.

We have attempted here to describe some of the tests that various organizations have developed in order that you might set goals in your skating. Each time you learn a new maneuver or trick, you can be sure there is some kind of test in which the trick or a variation of the trick will be asked for.

If you prefer not to take organized tests, you can make up your own in order to let yourself know if you are getting better in your skating. The simplest form of self-testing is to try a trick one day, then attempt the same trick the next time either longer, or higher if jumping is involved. Your skating will never be boring, in this way, since you are trying something different all the time. Besides, when you feel you have progressed far enough, you can take the AAU or USAC test or any of the Scouting tests and earn an award as well.

**Photographs representing the three branches of competitive skating.
(Top left) Speed skating. (Top right) Hockey. (Bottom) Artistic skating.**

44

CHAPTER SEVEN • COMPETITIVE SKATING

You may not have realized it when you watched skating on television, but the advanced skating you see in competitions is really three different versions of the maneuvers you learned early in your skating. First, there is **speed skating** which requires a high degree of skill and athletic ability in order to flash around a course at the speeds of present-day competitions. Then there is **hockey,** which in roller skating competition emphasizes the skating ability of the players rather than the violence associated with the professional ice sport. An international class hockey player is a superb athlete as well as a person who has mastered many skills on skates. Finally, the third type of competitive skating is **artistic,** the one that encompasses figure skating, dance skating and free skating. We'll discuss these later in the chapter, but you should be aware that all of the skills explained in earlier chapters are used in this part of the sport but with different degrees of expertise.

SPEED SKATING

Speed skating is a great way to enter competition against other skaters while being a good form of exercise as well. You will use a variation on the simple start that you learned back when you began to skate. Going around corners on a track will require you to use some form of the **cutting the corners** turn described in Chapter Four; and, of course, you will make yourself go by the same type of pushing that you used the first time you put on a pair of skates.

In other words, using the basic maneuvers you learned when you started, you can very quickly get active in competitive speed skating without having to learn a large number of new and complicated maneuvers. Speed skating contests are held both outdoors and indoors on surfaces such as terrazo, wood and plastic. There are local contests, statewide contests, national and international contests as well. If you like to move fast, speed skating is an excellent way to enter competition because you are sure to find a level of competition equal to your talents and experience.

In the outdoor finals of an Open Men's Five Mile Race, competitors are tightly bunched as they ready to **cut the corner**.

ROLLER HOCKEY

If you prefer team sports to individual contests, **roller hockey** is the way to go. There are many ways to play the game, one is exactly like ice hockey (except on wheels). In that version of the game, you would have sticks similar to ice hockey sticks and you would move a hard rubber puck around the surface, attempting to get it in a net or cage at one end of the playing surface. While you are doing this, members of the other team will be attempting to keep you from getting the puck into the net and at the same time bring the puck to a net at the other end (yours) of the playing surface.

Under international rules, roller hockey is played with a hard ball instead of a puck. The sticks are smaller and are curved at the end similar to field hockey sticks. (See the photographs for action shots from this version of hockey.)

The object is to pass the ball from player to player, all the while trying to maneuver away from your opponent so that you can get a shot at the net or goal. Playing roller hockey involves combining the many maneuvers we talked about in earlier chapters with the ability to control the ball with the curved stick.

You will find yourself having to skate forward, backward, cross over to turn to the left and the right, stopping both to the left and right, plus short spurts of very high speed skating. In order to shoot the ball, both forehand and backhand, it involves practicing the wrist motion which governs the speed and accuracy of the shot.

Whether you decide to organize a hockey game among your friends or you join an existing team, your participation in this game will give you an opportunity to make use of all the skills of skating plus to get plenty of exercise.

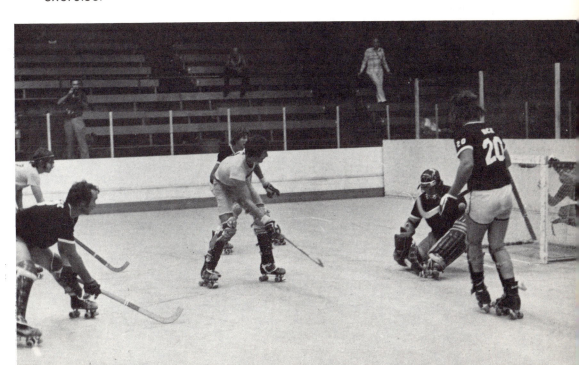

ARTISTIC SKATING

The **artistic skating** divisions are broken into three classes — **figure skating, dance skating** and **free style skating.**

Figure skating is done by one person at a time, **dance skating** requires two people skating together, while **free style** skating can be done by either one or two people at one time. Your choice of which kind of artistic skating you attempt can be decided by which appeals more to you since the tricks and maneuvers used in each have about the same degree of difficulty.

FIGURE SKATING

Figure Skating is that part of the sport where you show your control of your skate by attempting many tricks and maneuvers, all the time staying as close to a circle that has been drawn on the skating surface as is possible.

One of the earliest maneuvers described to you was the **figure 8.** This maneuver involved two circles. You skated on one foot around one circle, then switched to the other foot around the other circle.

Here, two young women perform **figure 8**s while skating backward. (Burns Photo)

50

Many variations of the basic **figure 8** are found in figure skating competition. For one, you can start in the circle to your right, skate around the circle on your right foot, and then step on your left taking you into the left circle. To do this, lean to the right on the right foot and lean to the left on the left foot. As a result, when you were on the right foot, your weight was on the right side of the foot which is the outside of the foot. This maneuver is called an **outside edge** because you lean to the outside of the foot. Of course, the same thing applies when you skate on your left foot. You lean to the left and therefore lean on the outside of the left foot.

Now, let's try something different. Skate in the left circle on the right foot followed by the right circle on the left foot. To do this, you lean to the left when skating on the right foot and lean to the right when skating on the left foot. You are then leaning on the inside of your foot, and we call the maneuver an **inside edge.**

Having mastered the first two figures, the next step is to try the **serpentine**. Here you will use a total of three circles, instead of two. Begin on the right foot skating to the right with two of the three circles to your right. When you have traversed one-half of the circle, you will arrive at the point where the next circle joins the one on which you are skating. Up to this point, you have been leaning to the right while skating on the right foot. You now change your lean to the left so that your right skate will start moving to the left and on into the next circle. Continue around this circle until you return to the point where you changed direction.

On your right skate, you will have rolled through one-half of a circle plus one full circle. This is now where you change feet.

Push yourself forward on your left foot, leaning to the right so you travel in the circle to your right. Continue for one-half of a circle until you come to where the next circle joins the one on which you are skating. Now change your lean to the left and go all the way around the circle on the left foot. You will now be back where you started from and can repeat the whole maneuver.

When being judged in **figure skating**, many points are considered. The way you hold your body position while you do the figure, how close to the line you skate, and how smoothly you execute are just a few of the factors looked at by the judges.

There are many figures but all are variations of the three figures described. Some are forward, some are backward, some involve turns made on one foot while doing the figure, but all evolve from three basic figures.

DANCE SKATING

Dance skating involves two people, skating as a couple, doing a prescribed set of steps to music. Just as in ballroom dancing, all types of music are used from foxtrots through waltzes, cha cha's, tangos and rhumbas — even disco. Because of the glide of your roller skates, you can add graceful motion to the normal rhythm of dancing.

Let's briefly look at some basic dances to see how we would do them. The first that comes to mind is the **Glide Waltz.** This is a dance in which both partners do the same steps side-by-side, skating forward at all times. The lady skates on the right side with the man at her left. The man's right hand extends behind the lady's back and holds her right hand at her waist on her right side. The man's left hand holds the lady's left hand in front of his chest.

Robert and Cathy Hayduk, 1976 Elementary Pairs Champs from Brookpark, Ohio, here demonstrate the proper position for the **Glide Waltz.**

Now we're ready to begin. Both partners will do a series of steps that make them glide to the left — a step on the left foot leaning to the left where the right foot is taken off the skating surface in back, followed by a step called a **chasse.**

A **chasse** is made on the right foot, continuing to lean to the left, but the left foot coming off the surface is held alongside in the air rather than letting it go in back the way the first step was skated. A third step is now skated again on the left foot, still leaning to the left, but once again the right foot coming off the surface is allowed to go back.

We began this section by mentioning that dancing on skates consists of doing maneuvers to music. At this point, we should consider how we apply the three steps just described to the music. The music used is waltz time. This means that it can be counted one-two-three, one-two-three. When doing the steps of the **Glide Waltz**, the first (left foot) is skated for two counts, the second (right chasse) is skated for one beat, and the third step (left foot again) is skated for three beats.

Now we have begun the Waltz by skating three steps which took us to the left. We continue the dance by skating the same three types of steps, except that we skate to the right and begin the first step on the right, leaning to the right. This is followed by a short, one beat step, on the left, during which we continue to lean to the right. Finally, we take another step on the right, this time for three beats of music, continuing to lean to the right.

We now have skated six steps — three leaning and rolling to the left, followed by three leaning and rolling to the right. You could continue to repeat these three steps in each direction for as long as you have space. In actual practice, however, there are usually limits to the area in which you skate. Either a school yard, or a skating rink, has fences or wall and it becomes necessary to alter your travel so you don't run into these limits. The way we do this is to skate a different set of steps called **corner steps.**

The **corner steps** of the **Glide Waltz** are very similar to the ones already discussed. You first step on the left foot for two beats of music, leaning to the left. That is followed by the right chasse step, continuing to lean to the left. Once more, you step on the left foot for three beats of music, leaning to the left, and letting the right foot extend in back of you.

Now you do something different. You place the right foot on the surface continuing to lean to the left and letting the left foot extend in back. This new step is skated for three beats of music. You can then either do the first set of three steps heading to the left, followed by a second set of three steps heading to the right, if there is room ahead of you. If you need to turn around more, you can repeat the corner steps. Thus, by selecting the combinations of the first, second and third set of steps, you can skate the **Glide Waltz** on any size surface.

Another dance, which in many ways seems similar, is called the **Society Blues.** Foxtrot or blues-rhythm music is used. This is counted in a one-two-three-four, one-two-three-four sequence. Once again, we have steps that are used to dance along a straight path such as one side of a skating rink or one side of a school yard. These are followed by a set of corner steps to turn you around when you run out of a straightaway.

Partners skate in the same position as the Glide Waltz — lady to the right of the man, both doing the same steps. This position is here demonstrated by Senior Dance Champions John LaBriola and Debra Coyne.

You begin the **Society Blues** by stepping on the left foot, leaning to the left, for just one beat of music. This is followed by stepping on the right foot, continuing to lean to the left and again holding this step for only one beat of music.

56

The third step of the **Society Blues** is again on the left foot, still leaning to the left and this step is held for two beats. These three steps together are called a **run** to the left because that is what it will feel like and look like when you skate the three steps to the music.

At this point, you have to choose whether to continue in the same general direction or go around a corner. If you plan to continue in the direction you are heading, the next step is on the right foot, leaning to the right, and holding it for four beats of music. Notice that the first three steps took four beats of music while the fourth step also took four beats of music. Thus, four beats were for skating to the left and four beats for skating to the right. By doing these four steps together, you will end up heading one one general direction by going both to the left and right.

To turn a corner or change direction, you do the corner steps which start the same as the steps just mentioned. A step on the left foot, leaning to the left, for one beat of music. A second step on the right, still leaning to the left, and again for one beat of music, followed by a step on the left again, for two beats of music. Now you skate a new step called a **cross under** or **cross back.** To do this, place your right foot on the surface in back of and crossed behind the left foot. This makes the left foot come off the surface in front of you. During this step, continue to lean to the left and hold the step for two beats of music. Thus, all of these steps tend to turn you around toward the left. By varying from corner steps to straightaway steps, you can do this dance anywhere and keep going as long as there is music to dance to.

There are over fifty dances that have been created, written and are published in book form by organizations such as the U.S.A. Confederation of Amateur Roller Skaters. These dances can be skated to all types of music and provide unlimited enjoyment.

FREE STYLE SKATING

Free style skating is the part of artistic skating in which you have the most opportunity to express your own ideas in skating. Whether you are skating by yourself or with a partner, you try **tricks** which involve **spinning, jumping** and fancy steps which are called **footwork.** As the name implies, you do whatever seems best to you for the mood you wish to convey. Music is very often used to help create the mood and give a rhythm to the program but free style can be practiced without music during the time you are learning some of the maneuvers.

One of the maneuvers that can be skated throughout a free style program is a **spin.** In another chapter, we discussed how to attempt a spin which called for turning around on two feet in a very small circle.

As you get better at it, you will find that you can spin on one foot, as Karlheing Losch of West Germany is doing in the photograph to the right.

In artistic skating, almost all spins are on one foot just as most maneuvers in all phases of artistic skating are on one foot.

Let us discuss one advanced type of spin called the **outside forward camel.** Going back to figure skating, you'll remember that in one figure, you skated on your right foot leaning to the right which made you curve around the circle to your right. To begin the **outside forward camel,** step out on your right foot leaning to the right and lifting your left foot off the surface to the back of you, then extending it as far back as you can stretch it while you lower your body from the waist up so you are almost horizontal. Press on your heel, which will allow your toe to begin to slide sideways and the spin will begin. Initially you will not have much speed, but as you learn to extend your left foot more and more, you will develop greater speed.

The skater pictured above is executing an **outside forward camel** starting on his left foot. Notice how his body is lowered from the waist up so he is almost horizontal.

As you can see, the spin is not a very easy maneuver and, frankly, should not be attempted by anyone until they have a fair amount of skating experience. There are many variations of the spin such as leaning to the left on the right foot, known as **inside forward camel** and, of course, all spins can be done while the skate is going backward. Thus, once again, skating provides many variations which prevents practice from becoming boring.

The maneuver which is most exciting for people to watch is the **jump.** In basic jumping, you attempted to use both feet to take off and you landed on both feet. In advanced free style skating, you skate on one foot, jump into the air, turn around while in the air, then land on one foot. Depending on which direction you turn in the air, and which foot you jump and land on, you will be doing one of some thirty different jumps. These have names like **waltz, flip, loop, mapes, lutz, axle** or **boekel.**

The **waltz jump** is executed by skating on the left foot, leaning to the left, then jumping into the air and turning to the left while in the air, so that you land skating backward on the right foot. You actually make a half turn in the air.

Some jumps have as many as three turns in the air and are called **triple jumps,** but they are exactly the same as a single jump except for the turns.

CHAPTER EIGHT • HORIZONS UNLIMITED

Competitive skating at the national and international levels provides a relatively few highly-proficient skaters with unlimited potential for satisfaction plus the thrill of representing the United States in international meets.

No 'street skater' can hope to achieve the skating skills necessary to enter such competitions and most have no inclination to do so. Acquiring such skills involves a considerable amount of money for professional instruction, as many as forty hours a week spent in practice, plus stern physical and mental disciplines.

Competition in this area is in **artistic** (**dance, figure** and **free style**), **speed** and **hockey** and — like other sports — demands a commitment which only a few are willing to make.

Dance, **figure** and **free style** skating at the rink level can be compared to the art of dance. These types of skating give the sport a new dimension for the participant wishing to devote more time in return for more enjoyment.

Speed skating is as natural to the average person as foot racing and offers the satisfaction of achievement in competition with fellow skaters.

Roller hockey emphasizes team play and skating ability while allowing each skater to share in the action.

Figure skating is the sport of moving the body around in a circle or semi-circle with a single stroke and with apparent ease and grace while balanced on a skate.

Dance skating has the natural appeal of graceful physical motion to music.

Free style skating is the epitome of the art of skating inasmuch as it demands the stamina of the speed skater, the edge control of the figure skater and the rhythm of the dancer.

The competitive skater who wishes to go on to national and international competition is far removed from the average street or rink skater but believes the rewards are worth the effort.

Of course, not everyone wants to be a world champion. One of the nice things about roller skating is that it is fun and good exercise at whatever level of expertise you develop. Roller skating is fun after school in the playground, fun at your neighborhood rink, fun alone or with your friends. What more could you ask from a recreational sport?

ABOUT THE AUTHOR

Joseph F. Shevelson was born in Chicago where he now resides. A graduate of Yale University, Mr. Shevelson is Vice President of both Chicago Roller Skate Company and the Roller Skating Foundation of America. He and his wife, Katherine, have three children, Pinny, Courtney and Nina.